INVESTIGATING SOLAR ENERGY

SUPER COOL SCIENCE EXPERIMENTS

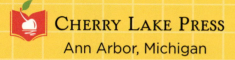
Cherry Lake Press
Ann Arbor, Michigan

by Christine Taylor-Butler

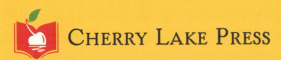

Published in the United States of America by
Cherry Lake Publishing Group
Ann Arbor, Michigan
www.cherrylakepublishing.com

Reading Adviser: Beth Walker Gambro, MS, Ed., Reading Consultant, Yorkville, IL

Content Editor: Robert Wolffe, EdD,
Professor of Teacher Education, Bradley University, Peoria, Illinois

Book Designer: Ed Morgan of Bowerbird Books

Photo Credits: cover, title page, © dee karen/Shutterstock; 4, 5, 9, 10, 13, 14, 17, 18, 21, 22, 25, 26, 28, 30, The Design Lab; 5, 6,7, freepik.com; 12, © RooftopStudioBangkok/Shutterstock; 16, © Spalnic/Shutterstock; 20, © violetkaipa/Shutterstock; 24, © New Africa/Shutterstock, 24

Copyright © 2026 by Cherry Lake Publishing

All rights reserved. No part of this book may be reproduced or utilized in any form or by any means without written permission from the publisher.

Cherry Lake Press is an imprint of Cherry Lake Publishing Group.

Library of Congress Cataloging-in-Publication Data has been filed and is available at catalog.loc.gov

Printed in the United States of America

A Note to Parents and Teachers:
Please review the instructions for these experiments before your children do them. Be sure to help them with any experiments you do not think they can safely conduct on their own.

A Note to Kids:
Be sure to ask an adult for help with these experiments when you need it. Always put your safety first!

Note from Publisher: Websites change regularly, and their future contents are outside of our control. Supervise children when conducting any recommended online searches for extended learning opportunities.

CONTENTS

Soak Up Some Sun!................................. 4

Getting Started.................................... 5

Experiment 1:..................................... 8
The Power of the Dark Side

Experiment 2:.................................... 12
What Color Is the Sun?

Experiment 3:.................................... 16
Clean Water from Solar Power

Experiment 4:.................................... 20
How Does Your Garden Grow?

Experiment 5:.................................... 24
Hot Dog!

Experiment 6:.................................... 28
Do It Yourself!

Glossary 30
For More Information 31
Index. 32
About the Author 32

Soak Up Some SUN!

It's big. It's blazing. What is it? The Sun! The Sun is nature's giant lightbulb. Have you ever stopped to really think about the Sun, or about how the Sun's energy affects something and can make it change forms?

If you've ever wondered about the Sun and its energy—and wanted to find out more—you are already one step closer to thinking like a scientist. In this book, we'll learn how scientists think. We'll do that by experimenting with **solar** energy, or energy from the Sun. We'll even learn how to design our own experiments. It's time to make some bright discoveries!

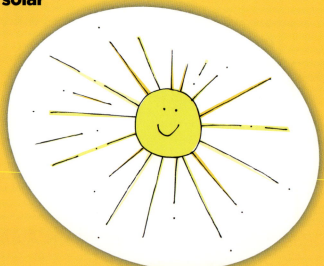

Getting STARTED

Scientists learn by studying something very carefully. For example, some scientists who study the Sun run experiments to see how light and heat affect Earth. They notice how sunlight is turned into energy that can be used by plants. Other scientists do experiments to see if the Sun's energy can replace the fuels we use.

Good scientists take notes on everything they discover. They record their **observations**. Sometimes those observations lead scientists to ask new questions. With new questions in mind, they design experiments to find the answers. Scientists usually work in labs. But most people don't have a lab. So we're going to do experiments with things you can find at home. Let's get started with some solar energy experiments!

5

When scientists design experiments, they often use the scientific method. What is the scientific method? It's a step-by-step process to answer specific questions. The steps don't always follow the same pattern. However, the scientific method often works like this:

STEP ONE: A scientist gathers the facts and makes observations about one particular thing.

STEP TWO: The scientist comes up with a question that is not answered by observations and facts.

STEP THREE: The scientist creates a **hypothesis**. This is a statement about what the scientist thinks might be the answer to the question.

STEP FOUR: The scientist tests the hypothesis by designing an experiment to see whether the hypothesis is correct. Then the scientist carries out the experiment and writes down what happens.

STEP FIVE: The scientist draws a **conclusion** based on the result of the experiment. The conclusion might be that the hypothesis is correct. Sometimes, though, the hypothesis is not correct. In that case, the scientist might develop a new hypothesis and another experiment.

In the following experiments, we'll see the scientific method in action. We'll gather some facts and observations about solar energy. And for each experiment, we'll develop a question and a hypothesis. Next, we'll do an actual experiment to see if our hypothesis is correct. By the end of the experiment, we should know something new about solar energy. Scientists, are you ready? Then let's go!

· EXPERIMENT 1 ·

The Power of the Dark Side

First, let's gather some observations. What do you already know about solar energy? You probably know that the Sun provides light in the daytime. The Sun also provides heat that warms Earth. Scientists know that light is a form of energy that can change into heat, another form of energy. They also know that different colors **absorb** different amounts of light. Have you ever worn a dark outfit on a sunny day? Did you feel very warm?

This leads to another question: Why do some colors make us feel hotter in sunlight than others? Could some colors absorb more light than others? Think about it. Here is a possible hypothesis for our first experiment: **Darker colors absorb more sunlight than lighter colors.**

Here's what you'll need:

- 2 paintbrushes
- 2 clear plastic bottles
- A container of black paint
- A container of white paint
- A black balloon
- A white balloon
- A sunny window

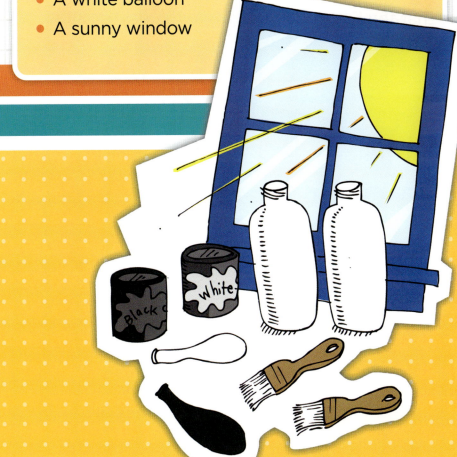

INSTRUCTIONS

1. Use a paintbrush to completely paint one bottle black.
2. Paint the other bottle white using the second paintbrush.
3. Set the bottles aside to dry.
4. After the paint has dried, attach the opening of the black balloon to the neck of the black bottle.
5. Attach the white balloon to the neck of the white bottle.
6. Set the bottles on a sunny windowsill. Wait 10 minutes. Observe what happens to the balloons.

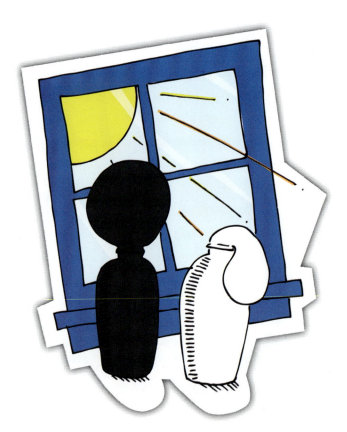

CONCLUSION

What happened to the balloons after the bottles sat in the Sun? Did they inflate? Did both fill with air? Which balloon started to inflate first?

Dark colors absorb more light than they **reflect**. The opposite is true of light colors. Sunlight is made up of different wavelengths. These show up as colors. When an object absorbs all of the colors, our eyes see the color black. When all of the colors of light are reflected, or bounced back, from an object, it looks white. Remember that light can be changed into heat. So the darker bottle absorbed more solar energy than the lighter one. That energy then heated the air inside the bottle. The heated air expanded and inflated the balloon. Was your hypothesis correct?

FACTS!

Ever wondered why the seasons change? You probably know our planet is a globe. It's also tilted on its axis. When Earth orbits the Sun, the part of the planet angled toward the Sun receives more direct rays. This affects temperature. More direct rays equal higher temperatures. Less direct rays equal lower temperatures. During winter in the Northern Hemisphere, that half of the globe is angled away from the Sun. During summer in the Northern Hemisphere, that half of the globe is angled toward the Sun. The equator gets the most direct rays. It stays warm year-round.

EXPERIMENT 2

What Color Is the Sun?

We learned from Experiment #1 that solar energy heats dark colors more than light colors. This explains why black seats in a car feel very hot in the summer, but beige seats do not. Let's take our findings from the last experiment a step further. What about specific colors? Do different colors absorb sunlight at different rates? Here is a new hypothesis: **Color can change the amount of heat that is absorbed by an object.**

Here's what you'll need:

- 7 clear plastic cups that are the same size
- A ruler
- Scissors
- 6 sheets of colored construction paper: one each of black, white, red, blue, green, and yellow
- Tape
- 7 ice cubes that are the same size
- A timer
- A piece of paper and a pencil
- A sunny window

· INSTRUCTIONS ·

1. Measure the height of your cups with a ruler.

2. Cut a strip from each sheet of colored paper that is the same height as the cups. The strips should also be long enough to completely wrap around the cups.

3. Use tape to secure 1 strip of colored paper around each cup. Use a different color for each cup. One cup will be left uncovered.

4. Cut a 4-inch (10.2-centimeter) square from each color of leftover construction paper. Cut larger squares if these don't completely cover the top of each cup.

5. Place 1 ice cube in each cup. Then place each square on top of the cup that is wrapped with the same color paper. The clear cup of ice will not be covered with paper.

6. Place the cups near a sunny window. Wait 1 minute. Use the timer to keep track of the time. After 1 minute, peek inside each cup. Have the ice cubes started to melt? If so, how much of each ice cube has melted? You can use your ruler to measure the height of the water. Record your observations.

7. Check the progress once every minute for 15 minutes. Record how much water has melted each time. How many minutes does it take each sample to completely melt?

CONCLUSION

Which ice cube melted the fastest? Which colored cup was it in? Which ice cube melted slowest? How did the results of the colored cups compare to the cup that was not covered in paper? Do different colors absorb solar energy at different rates? Remember that light energy can be changed into heat energy when absorbed by a color. This heat is what helps melt the ice. If the ice melted at different rates, does that mean the cups produced different amounts of heat? Was your hypothesis correct?

FACTS!

Sunlight is made up of waves. The more energy a wave has, the faster it moves. When sunlight hits water droplets in the sky, the light waves bend at different angles. The more energy a light wave has, the more it bends. This causes the light to separate into different colors. The bands of color are red, orange, yellow, green, blue, indigo, and violet. The result of this process is a rainbow.

EXPERIMENT 3

Clean Water from Solar Power

In Experiment #2, solar energy heated the ice cubes and turned them into liquid. If the Sun's energy had heated the water long enough, the water would have disappeared into the air as vapor. This process is called **evaporation**.

You have probably noticed a muddy puddle on the ground. Have you ever paid attention to raindrops that fall from the sky? Do the drops look clear or dirty? What's going on here? Could the

water in those clean drops have started out as dirty water on Earth? Do solar energy and evaporation play a role in this process? Come up with a hypothesis. Here is a possibility: **Solar energy can make dirty water clean.**

Here's what you'll need:

- Salt, coarse black pepper, sugar, and other spices
- 1 tablespoon of soil
- A spoon
- A large glass filled with water
- A coffee cup
- A clear mixing bowl
- Plastic food wrap
- Rubber bands
- A small rock
- A sunny window

INSTRUCTIONS

1. Mix the salt, pepper, sugar, spices, and soil into the water in the glass. Stir until it is no longer clear.

2. Place the coffee cup in the center of the mixing bowl.

3. Pour the dirty water into the bowl until it reaches just below the rim of the cup. Do not get water inside the cup.

4. Cover the bowl with plastic wrap. Do not stretch it tight. It should give a little. Poke the plastic wrap with your finger in the area above the empty cup to make a dip. Don't poke all the way through. Use rubber bands to hold the plastic wrap against the sides of the bowl.

5. Place the rock in the dip of the plastic wrap as a weight. The plastic wrap should dip down toward the cup, but not touch it.

6. Set the bowl next to a sunny window. Wait 1 hour. What is happening inside the bowl? Check the bowl again in 24 hours. Has something changed? Record your observations.

·CONCLUSION·

Solar energy heated the water molecules. Some of the water evaporated and became a vapor. When this vapor hit the plastic, it cooled and turned back into a liquid. This process is called **condensation**. The spices and soil are solids and cannot turn into vapor at these temperatures. They remained in the bowl. The water that dripped into the cup was clean. Was your hypothesis correct?

FACTS!

Rain is made when solar energy heats water on Earth. When water evaporates, the vapor rises into the air. Droplets form as the water vapor cools and comes into contact with bits of dust in the air. Many droplets help make up clouds. Eventually, the drops in clouds become too heavy. The liquid falls back to Earth as rain or snow or in some other form. This entire process is called the water cycle. Solar energy is the main source of fuel for this cycle.

EXPERIMENT 4

How Does Your Garden Grow?

The Sun's energy affects everything on Earth. We know, for instance, that farmers plant crops in places with sunlight. This might lead you to another question. What happens to some forms of life if there is no sunlight? Think about green plants and sunlight as you come up with a hypothesis. A possible hypothesis is: **Green plants need sunlight to stay healthy and grow.**

Here's what you'll need:

- 2 glass jars that are the same size
- Small pebbles
- Potting soil
- 2 small green plants that are the same kind and size (bean plants work well)
- Water
- A sunny window
- A dark closet

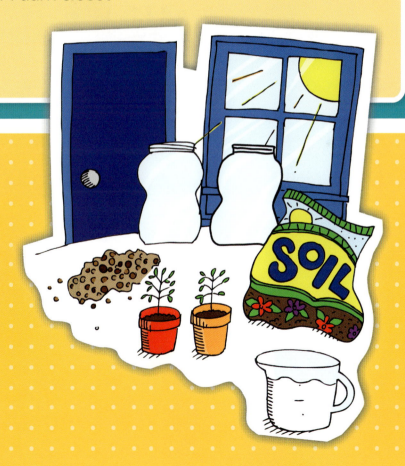

INSTRUCTIONS

1. Fill each jar with a 1-inch (2.5-cm) layer of pebbles.

2. Pour 2 inches (5.1 cm) of soil on top of the pebbles in each jar.

3. Make a small hole in the soil for the roots and place one plant in each jar. Add water to each jar until the soil is moist. Make sure the soil stays moist throughout the experiment.

4. Place one jar near a sunny window. Place the other jar in a warm, dark closet.

5. Look at each jar every day for 10 days. Observe the plants. How do they look? Study the plants at the same time of day each day.

CONCLUSION

Green plants are amazing. They can make their own food and give off oxygen in a process called photosynthesis. They use water and carbon dioxide to produce sugar. Where does the energy to do this come from? Sunlight, or solar energy! Some types of plants like to grow in shady areas. But all green plants contain a special green substance called chlorophyll that helps them use the Sun's energy. Light reflects off of the chlorophyll in plant cells to make plants appear green. Without light, the leaves appear pale. Does this explain your findings? Was your hypothesis correct?

FACTS!

Have you ever seen a field of sunflowers? A lot of people think that the movement of sunflowers is caused by the Sun. But 2016 and 2021 studies from the University of California, Davis, found that this isn't the case. Growing sunflowers have their own **circadian rhythms.** This means that their internal clocks tell them when to face in what direction. They still need sunlight to grow! When the Sun rises in the east, a growing sunflower faces east. When the sun sets in the west, a growing sunflower faces west. Once the plant fully matures, the bloom faces east full-time.

EXPERIMENT 5

Hot Dog!

You may have heard the saying, "It's so hot you can fry an egg outside!" But is this really possible? You know that sunlight can sometimes make an object too hot to touch. You also learned that black absorbs the Sun's energy faster than other colors. Do you think solar energy can cook something? Think of a hypothesis. Here are two options you might want to test. Choose the one you think is correct:

Hypothesis #1: Sunlight contains enough energy to cook food.

Hypothesis #2: Sunlight does not contain enough energy to cook food.

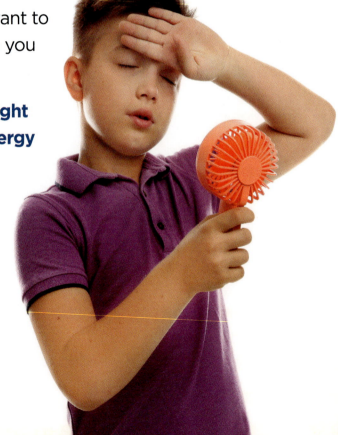

Here's what you'll need:

- A clean, empty pizza box
- A marker
- A ruler
- Scissors
- Aluminum foil
- Glue
- Clear plastic wrap
- Masking tape
- Black construction paper
- A hot dog or veggie dog
- An outdoor thermometer
- An oven or baking thermometer
- A timer

· INSTRUCTIONS ·

1. Draw a square on the top of the pizza box using a marker. The edges of the pizza box should be 2 inches (5.1 cm) from each side of the square.

2. Carefully cut along the sides and front of the square with the scissors to make a flap. Carefully lift the flap until it is vertical.

3. Cut a piece of aluminum foil that is large enough to cover the inside of the flap. Make sure the shinier side of the foil is facing you. Glue it in place.

4. Under the flap, cover the hole in the top of the box with plastic wrap. Stretch it tight. Tape the edges of the plastic wrap down.

5. For the inside of the pizza box, cut a piece of aluminum foil large enough to cover the bottom and inner sides. Smooth any wrinkles, and then glue the foil to the inside of the box, shiny side up. Place the sheet of black construction paper on top of the foil

that is on the base of the pizza box. You've made a solar oven!

6. Place a hot dog or veggie dog in the middle of your oven. Set your oven outside in a hot, sunny spot.

7. Measure the outside temperature with the outdoor thermometer and write it on a piece of paper. Place the oven thermometer inside your box.

8. Close the pizza box. Open the flap so that the Sun's rays hit the foil on the flap and shine through the plastic into the bottom of your box. It may take some time to get this set up just right. Use tape to keep the flap in the correct position, if necessary.

9. Use your timer to check your solar oven every 15 minutes for 1 hour. Be careful that you don't burn yourself!

CONCLUSION

Check the thermometer after several minutes. How hot did it get inside the solar oven? Were you able to cook the hot dog? If so, how long did it take? The foil on the flap reflected and concentrated the sunlight through the plastic and into the pizza box. The black paper helped absorb this sunlight. The plastic helped prevent the heat from escaping. Was your hypothesis correct?

EXPERIMENT 6

Do It Yourself!

Wasn't making a solar oven to cook food exciting? It sure was! But don't stop there. Come up with another experiment using a solar oven. What would happen if you changed the color of the construction paper inside the oven? Or replaced the shiny foil with white paper? Would that affect your results? What if you tried to use the oven during different times of the day? Is it possible to cook an egg or melt a marshmallow with your solar oven?

These are all great questions. Come up with a hypothesis. Then design and run an experiment. Record your observations and state your conclusion. Now that you can think like a scientist, you can see that solar energy really is hot stuff!

FACTS!

The Sun is more than 92 million miles (148 million km) away. But its light and energy can reach Earth in 8 minutes. Only a tiny amount of the Sun's energy reaches Earth. Even so, more solar energy reaches the United States in one hour than all the other sources of fuel used by humans in a year. The Sun is a great source of **renewable energy**. Many people use **solar collectors** and solar cells to heat and power buildings. Solar cells are objects that turn sunlight into electricity. Your pizza box oven is a type of solar collector.

Glossary

absorb (uhb-ZORB) to take in

circadian rhythms (suhr-KAY-dee-uhn RIH-thuhmz) physical, mental, or behavioral changes that happen in a 24-hour cycle

conclusion (kuhn-KLOO-zhuhn) a final thought, or opinion

condensation (kahn-den-SAY-shuhn) the process in which a gas changes to a liquid or solid

evaporation (ih-vaa-puh-RAY-shuhn) the process in which a liquid changes to a gas or vapor

hypothesis (hahy-POTH-uh-sis) a logical guess about what will happen in an experiment

observations (ahb-suhr-VAY-shuhnz) things that are seen or noticed with one's senses

reflect (rih-FLEKT) to bounce or send back light rays, sound, or heat from a surface

renewable energy (rih-NOO-uh-buhl EH-nuhr-jee) energy from a source that does not run out; wind and solar power are examples

solar (SOH-luhr) having to do with the Sun or powered by the Sun's energy

solar collectors (SOH-luhr kuh-LEK-tuhrz) devices that collect and concentrate heat energy from the Sun and turn it into useful forms of energy

For More Information

BOOKS

Bunting, Philip. *Super Power.* San Francisco, CA: Bright Light Books via Chronicle Books, 2024.

Huggett, Audrey. *Solar Energy Projects.* Makers as Innovators. Ann Arbor, MI: Cherry Lake Publishing, 2016.

Twamley, Erin. Joshua Sneideman. Micah Rauch (illustrator). *Renewable Energy: Power the World with Sustainable Fuel with Hand-On Science Activities for Kids.* Norwich, VT: Nomad Press, 2024.

WEBSITES

Explore these online sources with an adult:

Does Solar Energy Work? Video | Octopus Energy | YouTube

The Environment: Solar Energy | Ducksters

What Is Solar Energy? | Earth.org Kids

Index

absorption, 8, 11–12, 15, 24, 27–28
absorption experiments, 8–15, 24–27
air, 11, 16, 19

carbon dioxide, 23
clean water experiment, 16–19
colors, 8, 11–13, 15, 28
colors experiments, 8–15
conclusions, 6, 11, 15, 19, 23, 27, 29
condensation, 19
condensation experiment, 16–19
cooking experiments, 24–29

do-it-yourself experiment, 28–29

electricity, 29
evaporation, 16–17
evaporation experiment, 16–19

heat, 5, 8, 11–12, 15–16, 19, 27, 29
heat experiments, 8–15, 24–29
hypotheses, 6–8, 11–12, 15, 17, 19–20, 23–24, 27, 29

light, 4–5, 8, 10–12, 15, 23, 29
light experiment, 20–23
light waves, 15

notes, 5

observations, 5–8, 14, 19, 29

photosynthesis, 23
plants, 20–23
plants experiment, 20–23

questions, 5–8, 20, 29

rainbows, 15

scientific method, 6–7
scientists, 4–8, 29
solar cells, 29
solar collectors, 29
sunflowers, 23

water cycle, 19

About the Author

Christine Taylor-Butler is an author with degrees in both civil engineering and art and design from MIT. When Christine is not writing, she is reading, drawing, or looking for unusual new science ideas to try. She is the author of more than 90 fiction and nonfiction books for children.